THE WORLD OF RIDDLES FOR PRESCHOOLERS

Reading and Writing Books for Kids
Children's Reading and Writing Books

BABY PROFESSOR

EDUCATION KIDS

Speedy Publishing LLC
40 E. Main St. #1156
Newark, DE 19711
www.speedypublishing.com
Copyright 2017

WHAT AM I?

LET ME TELL YOU
SOMETHING ABOUT MYSELF.
THEN SEE IF YOU CAN GUESS
WHAT I AM.

READ EACH OF THE RIDDLES BELOW.
WRITE A WORD FROM THE BOX ON THE LINE
TO ANSWER EACH OF THE RIDDLES.

I am hot.
I live in the sky.
I am bright.
Don't look straight at me.
I disappear in the night.

_____

- - - - - - - - - - - - - - - - - - - -

_____

I live in the water.
You can drive me.
I might make you sick.
Don't put a hole in me.
Tie me up when you're done.

_____

- - - - - - - - - - - - - - - - - - - -

_____

boat

sun

READ EACH OF THE RIDDLES BELOW. WRITE A WORD FROM THE BOX ON THE LINE TO ANSWER EACH OF THE RIDDLES.

I am in your body.
I am red.
I am the symbol for love.
Blood pumps through me.
Please don't break me.

_____

- - - - - - - - - - - - - - -

_____

I am red, green, or yellow.
I am a healthy snack.
I make good juice.
You can bite me or slice me.
Give me to a teacher.

_____

- - - - - - - - - - - - - - -

_____

apple

heart

**READ EACH OF THE RIDDLES BELOW.
WRITE A WORD FROM THE BOX ON THE LINE
TO ANSWER EACH OF THE RIDDLES.**

I am circular.
I go up and down.
You can throw me.
You can catch me.
Be careful with me near
windows.

_____

_____

I cry a lot.
I love milk.
Everyone smiles at me.
Please pick me up.
I'm new to the world.

_____

_____

ball

baby

READ EACH OF THE RIDDLES BELOW. WRITE A WORD FROM THE BOX ON THE LINE TO ANSWER EACH OF THE RIDDLES.

I am usually green and brown.
I can live for a long time.
I'm a house for a bird.
Kids love to climb me.
I need rain.

_____

- - - - - - - - - - - - - - - - -

_____

I smell nice.
I am beautiful.
I come in many different colors.
You can pick me.
Don't forget to water me.

_____

- - - - - - - - - - - - - - - - -

_____

tree

flower

READ EACH OF THE RIDDLES BELOW.
WRITE A WORD FROM THE BOX ON THE LINE
TO ANSWER EACH OF THE RIDDLES.

I have five wheels.
You need a key for me.
You can sit inside me.
Don't make me go too fast.
Please wear my belt.

_____

I twinkle.
There are millions of me.
I will light your way.
I come out at night.
I hide in the city.

_____

star

car

READ EACH OF THE RIDDLES BELOW. WRITE A WORD FROM THE BOX ON THE LINE TO ANSWER EACH OF THE RIDDLES.

I use a long track.
I transport heavy loads.
Many tourists use me.
Watch for lights to stop for me.
I will show you beautiful scenery.

_____

Please blow air in me.
I come in many colors.
I'm a symbol of celebration.
Don't touch me with anything sharp.
I only last a day or two.

_____

train

ballon

READ EACH OF THE RIDDLES BELOW.
WRITE A WORD FROM THE BOX ON THE LINE
TO ANSWER EACH OF THE RIDDLES.

Children love to play with me.
I am not useful indoors.
Don't tangle my long string.
Look up and watch me dance.
Run if you want me to fly
faster.

_____

- - - - - - - - - - - - - - - - - - - -

_____

airplane

I am a safe ride.
I go very high in the sky.
You will get service on me.
You can watch a movie
inside me.
I might make your ears pop.

_____

- - - - - - - - - - - - - - - - - - - -

_____

kite

READ EACH OF THE RIDDLES BELOW.
WRITE A WORD FROM THE BOX ON THE LINE
TO ANSWER EACH OF THE RIDDLES.

I am usually made of
brick or wood.
I have many doors and windows.
I will keep you warm and cozy.
Sell me when your family grows.
Please clean me for visitors.

_____

- - - - - - - - - - - - - - - - - - - -

_____

house

I am paper's enemy.
Keep me away from small children.
You use me in art class.
I can change the style of your hair.
Please don't run with me in your
hands.

_____

- - - - - - - - - - - - - - - - - - - -

_____

scissors

READ EACH OF THE RIDDLES BELOW. WRITE A WORD FROM THE BOX ON THE LINE TO ANSWER EACH OF THE RIDDLES.

I will entertain you.
I tell funny and sad stories.
I am shaped like a cube.
I plug into the wall.
Many people fall asleep
watching me.

_____

- - - - - - - - - - - - - - - - - -

_____

The ocean is my real home.
Humans trick me to bite.
I am an easy pet to look after.
Gold is a common color of me.
I like to blow bubbles.

_____

- - - - - - - - - - - - - - - - - -

_____

fish

television

READ EACH OF THE RIDDLES BELOW.
WRITE A WORD FROM THE BOX ON THE LINE TO ANSWER EACH OF THE RIDDLES.

You don't always answer me.
I can connect you to the world.
I beep and ring.
You have to press my buttons.
Modern types of me are cordless.

_____

_____

I come in a pair.
You have to tie and untie me.
Don't go outside without me.
Take me off before you go in
the water.
I come in a very useful box.

_____

_____

telephone

shoes

READ EACH OF THE RIDDLES BELOW. WRITE A WORD FROM THE BOX ON THE LINE TO ANSWER EACH OF THE RIDDLES.

I am associated with Spring.
I love to hop in the grass.
I play in your vegetable garden.
My teeth are long and sharp.
I am soft to pet.

_____

_____

I am a home for royalty.
There are many of me in England.
I am made of stone.
I am protected by a ring of water.
I'm found in many legends.

_____

_____

rabbit

castle

READ EACH OF THE RIDDLES BELOW.
WRITE A WORD FROM THE BOX ON THE LINE
TO ANSWER EACH OF THE RIDDLES.

I have buttons or a zipper.
You don't need me in the summer.
Hang me in your front closet.
I'll protect you from a cold wind.
I have pockets and sometimes a belt.

_____

- - - - - - - - - - - - - -

_____

I am multi-colored.
I appear after a storm.
People always point at me.
Everyone takes my picture.
Legend says there is gold at
the bottom of me.

_____

- - - - - - - - - - - - - -

_____

coat

rainbow

READ EACH OF THE RIDDLES BELOW.
WRITE A WORD FROM THE BOX ON THE LINE
TO ANSWER EACH OF THE RIDDLES.

I am a delicious treat.
Lick me with your tongue.
I come in a bowl or a cone.
Don't eat me too slowly.
One of my flavours is vanilla.

_____

- -

_____

I'm a pretend animal.
I have four paws.
I'm stuffed with fluff.
Please take me to bed with you.
Hug me if you have a bad dream.

_____

- -

_____

teddy bear

ice cream

READ EACH OF THE RIDDLES BELOW. WRITE A WORD FROM THE BOX ON THE LINE TO ANSWER EACH OF THE RIDDLES.

I'll keep your hair dry.
Bring me just in case.
I'm long and light to carry.
Don't open me in the house.
I hope you don't need me today.

_____

I live in the jungle.
I love to eat bananas.
I'm very similar to a human.
I'm a curious creature.
I have a long curly tail.

_____

umbrella

monkey

READ EACH OF THE RIDDLES BELOW. WRITE A WORD FROM THE BOX ON THE LINE TO ANSWER EACH OF THE RIDDLES.

I am popular for winter sports.
I can be very dangerous.
You can go up or down me.
I get colder as you go higher.
Don't forget your safety gear.

_____

- -

_____

You use me when you're resting.
I protect your neck and head.
I'm soft and comfortable.
Ask for me on an airplane.
Fighting with me is fun.

_____

- -

_____

pillow

mountain

READ EACH OF THE RIDDLES BELOW. WRITE A WORD FROM THE BOX ON THE LINE TO ANSWER EACH OF THE RIDDLES.

I don't have eyes, ears, nose and tongue, but I can see, smell, hear and taste everything.

_____

- - - - - - - - - - - - - - -

_____

I do not have wings, but I can fly. I don't have eyes, but I will cry!

_____

- - - - - - - - - - - - - - -

_____

cloud

brain

READ EACH OF THE RIDDLES BELOW. WRITE A WORD FROM THE BOX ON THE LINE TO ANSWER EACH OF THE RIDDLES.

I do not speak, cannot hear or speak anything, but I will always tell the truth.

_____

- -

_____

I go around all the places, cities, towns and villages, but never come inside.

_____

- -

_____

mirror

street

READ EACH OF THE RIDDLES BELOW. WRITE A WORD FROM THE BOX ON THE LINE TO ANSWER EACH OF THE RIDDLES.

I have lots of memories, but I own nothing.

_____

- - - - - - - - - - - - - - - - - - -

_____

I have no legs. I will never walk, but always run.

_____

- - - - - - - - - - - - - - - - - - -

_____

river

photo frame

**READ EACH OF THE RIDDLES BELOW.
WRITE A WORD FROM THE BOX ON THE LINE
TO ANSWER EACH OF THE RIDDLES.**

I have no life, but I can die

_____

- -

_____

I have rivers, but do not have water. I have dense forests, but no trees and animals. I have cities, but no people live in those cities.

_____

- -

_____

battery

map

READ EACH OF THE RIDDLES BELOW. WRITE A WORD FROM THE BOX ON THE LINE TO ANSWER EACH OF THE RIDDLES.

I never ask questions, but always answered.

_____

- - - - - - - - - - - - - - - - -

_____

I was born big, but as the day passes, as I get older, I become small.

_____

- - - - - - - - - - - - - - - - -

_____

doorbell

candle

READ EACH OF THE RIDDLES BELOW. WRITE A WORD FROM THE BOX ON THE LINE TO ANSWER EACH OF THE RIDDLES.

I am full of keys, but I cannot open any door.

_____

- -

_____

If you give me water, I will die. What am I?

_____

- -

_____

Fire

piano

READ EACH OF THE RIDDLES BELOW. WRITE A WORD FROM THE BOX ON THE LINE TO ANSWER EACH OF THE RIDDLES.

Many times you need me. The more and more you take me further, the more and more you leave me behind.

_____

People buy me to eat, but never eat me.

_____

footsteps

plate

READ EACH OF THE RIDDLES BELOW.
WRITE A WORD FROM THE BOX ON THE LINE TO ANSWER EACH OF THE RIDDLES.

You will throw me away
when you want to use me.
You will take me in when you
don't want to use me.

_____

- - - - - - - - - - - - - - - -

_____

I have no bones and no legs,
but if you keep me warm, I
will soon walk away.

_____

- - - - - - - - - - - - - - - -

_____

egg

anchor

WHAT IS IT?

LET ME SHOW YOU
SOME PICTURE CLUES.
THEN SEE IF YOU CAN GUESS
WHAT IT IS.

USE THE PICTURE CLUES TO FIGURE OUT WHICH WORD COMPLETES EACH SENTENCE. CIRCLE THE CORRECT WORD AND THEN WRITE IT ON THE LINE.

I see the
SHOE
SHOVEL

_____

I see the
BAT
BOX

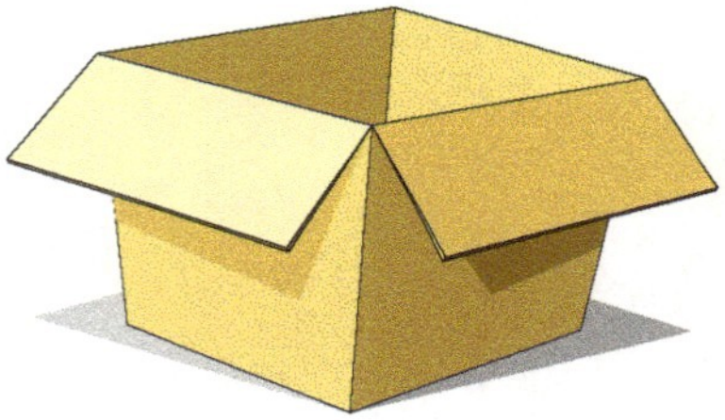

_____

I see the
HAT
HOLE

_____

USE THE PICTURE CLUES TO FIGURE OUT WHICH WORD COMPLETES EACH SENTENCE. CIRCLE THE CORRECT WORD AND THEN WRITE IT ON THE LINE.

I see the
ROPE
RING

_____

I see the
TREE
TENT

_____

I see the
ANT
APPLE

_____

USE THE PICTURE CLUES TO FIGURE OUT WHICH WORD COMPLETES EACH SENTENCE. CIRCLE THE CORRECT WORD AND THEN WRITE IT ON THE LINE.

I see the

BEAR

BEE

_____

I see the

CAR

CAT

_____

I see the

DOG

DONKEY

_____

USE THE PICTURE CLUES TO FIGURE OUT WHICH WORD COMPLETES EACH SENTENCE. CIRCLE THE CORRECT WORD AND THEN WRITE IT ON THE LINE.

I see the
DOVE
DUCK

_____

I see the
ENVELOPE
EGG

_____

I see the
ELEPHANT
EAGLE

_____

USE THE PICTURE CLUES TO FIGURE OUT WHICH WORD COMPLETES EACH SENTENCE. CIRCLE THE CORRECT WORD AND THEN WRITE IT ON THE LINE.

I see the
FISH
FROG

_____

I see the
FARMER
FLOWER

_____

I see the
GIFT
GOAT

_____

ANSWER KEY

READ EACH OF THE RIDDLES BELOW.
WRITE A WORD FROM THE BOX ON THE LINE
TO ANSWER EACH OF THE RIDDLES.

I am hot.
I live in the sky.
I am bright.
Don't look straight at me.
I disappear in the night.

_____
sun
- - - - - - - - - - - - - - - - - - - -
_____

I live in the water.
You can drive me.
I might make you sick.
Don't put a hole in me.
Tie me up when you're done.

_____
boat
- - - - - - - - - - - - - - - - - - - -
_____

boat

sun

READ EACH OF THE RIDDLES BELOW. WRITE A WORD FROM THE BOX ON THE LINE TO ANSWER EACH OF THE RIDDLES.

I am in your body.
I am red.
I am the symbol for love.
Blood pumps through me.
Please don't break me.

heart

I am red, green, or yellow.
I am a healthy snack.
I make good juice.
You can bite me or slice me.
Give me to a teacher.

apple

apple

heart

READ EACH OF THE RIDDLES BELOW. WRITE A WORD FROM THE BOX ON THE LINE TO ANSWER EACH OF THE RIDDLES.

I am circular.
I go up and down.
You can throw me.
You can catch me.
Be careful with me near windows.

I cry a lot.
I love milk.
Everyone smiles at me.
Please pick me up.
I'm new to the world.

ball

baby

READ EACH OF THE RIDDLES BELOW.
WRITE A WORD FROM THE BOX ON THE LINE
TO ANSWER EACH OF THE RIDDLES.

I am usually green and brown.
I can live for a long time.
I'm a house for a bird.
Kids love to climb me.
I need rain.

tree

I smell nice.
I am beautiful.
I come in many different colours.
You can pick me.
Don't forget to water me.

flower

tree

flower

READ EACH OF THE RIDDLES BELOW. WRITE A WORD FROM THE BOX ON THE LINE TO ANSWER EACH OF THE RIDDLES.

I have five wheels.
You need a key for me.
You can sit inside me.
Don't make me go too fast.
Please wear my belt.

car

I twinkle.
There are millions of me.
I will light your way.
I come out at night.
I hide in the city.

star

star

car

READ EACH OF THE RIDDLES BELOW.
WRITE A WORD FROM THE BOX ON THE LINE
TO ANSWER EACH OF THE RIDDLES.

I use a long track.
I transport heavy loads.
Many tourists use me.
Watch for lights to stop for me.
I will show you beautiful scenery.

train

Please blow air in me.
I come in many colours.
I'm a symbol of celebration.
Don't touch me with anything
sharp.
I only last a day or two.

ballon

train

ballon

READ EACH OF THE RIDDLES BELOW. WRITE A WORD FROM THE BOX ON THE LINE TO ANSWER EACH OF THE RIDDLES.

Children love to play with me.
I am not useful indoors.
Don't tangle my long string.
Look up and watch me dance.
Run if you want me to fly faster.

kite

I am a safe ride.
I go very high in the sky.
You will get service on me.
You can watch a movie inside me.
I might make your ears pop.

airplane

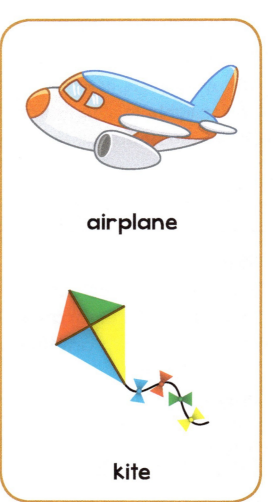

airplane

kite

READ EACH OF THE RIDDLES BELOW. WRITE A WORD FROM THE BOX ON THE LINE TO ANSWER EACH OF THE RIDDLES.

I am usually made of
brick or wood.
I have many doors and windows.
I will keep you warm and cozy.
Sell me when your family grows.
Please clean me for visitors.

house

I am paper's enemy.
Keep me away from small children.
You use me in art class.
I can change the style of your hair.
Please don't run with me in your
hands.

house

scissors

READ EACH OF THE RIDDLES BELOW.
WRITE A WORD FROM THE BOX ON THE LINE
TO ANSWER EACH OF THE RIDDLES.

I will entertain you.
I tell funny and sad stories.
I am shaped like a cube.
I plug into the wall.
Many people fall asleep
watching me.

television

The ocean is my real home.
Humans trick me to bite.
I am an easy pet to look after.
Gold is a common colour of me.
I like to blow bubbles.

fish

fish

television

READ EACH OF THE RIDDLES BELOW.
WRITE A WORD FROM THE BOX ON THE LINE
TO ANSWER EACH OF THE RIDDLES.

You don't always answer me.
I can connect you to the world.
I beep and ring.
You have to press my buttons.
Modern types of me are cordless.

telephone

telephone

I come in a pair.
You have to tie and untie me.
Don't go outside without me.
Take me off before you go in the water.
I come in a very useful box.

shoes

shoes

READ EACH OF THE RIDDLES BELOW.
WRITE A WORD FROM THE BOX ON THE LINE
TO ANSWER EACH OF THE RIDDLES.

I am associated with Spring.
I love to hop in the grass.
I play in your vegetable
garden.
My teeth are long and sharp.
I am soft to pet.

rabbit

I am a home for royalty.
There are many of me in England.
I am made of stone.
I am protected by a ring of water.
I'm found in many legends.

castle

rabbit

castle

READ EACH OF THE RIDDLES BELOW. WRITE A WORD FROM THE BOX ON THE LINE TO ANSWER EACH OF THE RIDDLES.

I have buttons or a zipper.
You don't need me in the summer.
Hang me in your front closet.
I'll protect you from a cold wind.
I have pockets and sometimes a belt.

coat

I am multi-coloured.
I appear after a storm.
People always point at me.
Everyone takes my picture.
Legend says there is gold at
the bottom of me.

rainbow

coat

rainbow

READ EACH OF THE RIDDLES BELOW.
WRITE A WORD FROM THE BOX ON THE LINE
TO ANSWER EACH OF THE RIDDLES.

I am a delicious treat.
Lick me with your tongue.
I come in a bowl or a cone.
Don't eat me too slowly.
One of my flavours is vanilla.

ice cream

I'm a pretend animal.
I have four paws.
I'm stuffed with fluff.
Please take me to bed with you.
Hug me if you have a bad dream.

teddy bear

teddy bear

ice cream

READ EACH OF THE RIDDLES BELOW. WRITE A WORD FROM THE BOX ON THE LINE TO ANSWER EACH OF THE RIDDLES.

I'll keep your hair dry.
Bring me just in case.
I'm long and light to carry.
Don't open me in the house.
I hope you don't need me today.

umbrella

I live in the jungle.
I love to eat bananas.
I'm very similar to a human.
I'm a curious creature.
I have a long curly tail.

monkey

umbrella

monkey

READ EACH OF THE RIDDLES BELOW. WRITE A WORD FROM THE BOX ON THE LINE TO ANSWER EACH OF THE RIDDLES.

I am popular for winter sports.
I can be very dangerous.
You can go up or down me.
I get colder as you go higher.
Don't forget your safety gear.

mountain

You use me when you're resting.
I protect your neck and head.
I'm soft and comfortable.
Ask for me on an airplane.
Fighting with me is fun.

pillow

pillow

mountain

READ EACH OF THE RIDDLES BELOW. WRITE A WORD FROM THE BOX ON THE LINE TO ANSWER EACH OF THE RIDDLES.

I don't have eyes, ears, nose and tongue, but I can see, smell, hear and taste everything.

brain

I do not have wings, but I can fly. I don't have eyes, but I will cry!

cloud

cloud

brain

READ EACH OF THE RIDDLES BELOW. WRITE A WORD FROM THE BOX ON THE LINE TO ANSWER EACH OF THE RIDDLES.

I do not speak, cannot hear or speak anything, but I will always tell the truth.

mirror

I go around all the places, cities, towns and villages, but never come inside.

street

mirror

street

READ EACH OF THE RIDDLES BELOW. WRITE A WORD FROM THE BOX ON THE LINE TO ANSWER EACH OF THE RIDDLES.

I have lots of memories, but I own nothing.

photo frame

I have no legs. I will never walk, but always run.

river

river

photo frame

**READ EACH OF THE RIDDLES BELOW.
WRITE A WORD FROM THE BOX ON THE LINE
TO ANSWER EACH OF THE RIDDLES.**

I have no life, but I can die

battery

I have rivers, but do not have water. I have dense forests, but no trees and animals. I have cities, but no people live in those cities.

map

battery

map

READ EACH OF THE RIDDLES BELOW. WRITE A WORD FROM THE BOX ON THE LINE TO ANSWER EACH OF THE RIDDLES.

I never ask questions, but always answered.

doorbell

doorbell

I was born big, but as the day passes, as I get older, I become small.

candle

candle

READ EACH OF THE RIDDLES BELOW. WRITE A WORD FROM THE BOX ON THE LINE TO ANSWER EACH OF THE RIDDLES.

I am full of keys, but I cannot open any door.

If you give me water, I will die. What am I?

Fire

piano

READ EACH OF THE RIDDLES BELOW. WRITE A WORD FROM THE BOX ON THE LINE TO ANSWER EACH OF THE RIDDLES.

Many times you need me. The more and more you take me further, the more and more you leave me behind.

footsteps

People buy me to eat, but never eat me.

plate

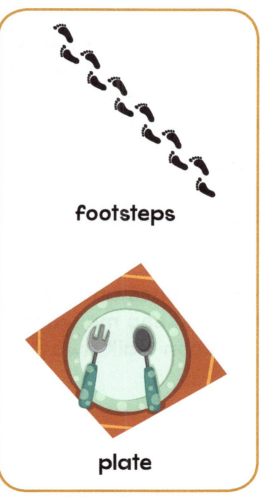

footsteps

plate

READ EACH OF THE RIDDLES BELOW. WRITE A WORD FROM THE BOX ON THE LINE TO ANSWER EACH OF THE RIDDLES.

You will throw me away when you want to use me. You will take me in when you don't want to use me.

anchor

I have no bones and no legs, but if you keep me warm, I will soon walk away.

egg

egg

anchor

USE THE PICTURE CLUES TO FIGURE OUT WHICH WORD COMPLETES EACH SENTENCE. CIRCLE THE CORRECT WORD AND THEN WRITE IT ON THE LINE.

I see the
(SHOE)
SHOVEL

shoe

I see the
BAT
(BOX)

box

I see the
(HAT)
HOLE

hat

USE THE PICTURE CLUES TO FIGURE OUT WHICH WORD COMPLETES EACH SENTENCE. CIRCLE THE CORRECT WORD AND THEN WRITE IT ON THE LINE.

I see the
ROPE
(RING)

ring

I see the
(TREE)
TENT

tree

I see the
ANT
(APPLE)

apple

USE THE PICTURE CLUES TO FIGURE OUT WHICH WORD COMPLETES EACH SENTENCE. CIRCLE THE CORRECT WORD AND THEN WRITE IT ON THE LINE.

I see the
BEAR
(BEE)

bee

I see the
(CAR)
CAT

car

I see the
(DOG)
DONKEY

dog

USE THE PICTURE CLUES TO FIGURE OUT WHICH WORD COMPLETES EACH SENTENCE. CIRCLE THE CORRECT WORD AND THEN WRITE IT ON THE LINE.

I see the
DOVE
(DUCK)

duck

I see the
ENVELOPE
(EGG)

egg

I see the
(ELEPHANT)
EAGLE

elephant

USE THE PICTURE CLUES TO FIGURE OUT WHICH WORD COMPLETES EACH SENTENCE. CIRCLE THE CORRECT WORD AND THEN WRITE IT ON THE LINE.

I see the
FISH
FROG

fish

I see the
FARMER
FLOWER

flower

I see the
GIFT
GOAT

gift

Visit

BABY PROFESSOR
EDUCATION KIDS

www.BabyProfessorBooks.com

to download Free Baby Professor eBooks
and view our catalog of new and exciting
Children's Books

CPSIA information can be obtained
at www.ICGtesting.com
Printed in the USA
LVHW060702290522
720020LV00023B/480